Collected Poems

Collected Poems

WILLIAM ROWE

For Aodan, Stephen, and Ulli

ISBN
978-1-326-64379-9

ISSN
2041 0948

CRATER 41

London Barcelona

November 2016

CONTENTS

Acknowledgements

Many thanks to Aodan McCardle for the cover.

Incisions was published by Iodine Press, Brighton, in 2014
Nation was first published by Klinamen, London, in 2012. An enlarged and revised edition was published by Knives, Forks, and Spoons, Newton-Le-Willows, in 2015.
The Earth Has Been Destroyed was published by Veer Books, London, in 2009.
Working the Signs was published as Spanner No. 30, edited by Allen Fisher, 1992.

Some of these poems were first published in *Veer Away*; *Veer Off*; *Ad ssing the future*; *A-a-a-a-a*; *Openned Anthology*; *Poetry and Revolution*; *International Egg and Poultry Review*, 2011, edited by Justin Katko and Luke Roberts; *Gathered Here Today: Celebrating Geraldine Monk at 60*, edited by Scott Thurston; *An Educated Desire: Robert Sheppard at 60*, edited by Scott Thurston; *Poems for Freedom*, Infinite Editions; *Vile products* (Sad Press), edited by Samantha Walton; *Veer Vier for Will Rowe*, edited by Carol Watts, Aodán McCardle and Stephen Mooney; *Hi Zero*, edited by Joe Luna; *London Rivers*, edited by Barbara Hardy.

Many thanks to the editors of all the above publications.

DEATH PURGE (2016)

death purge

so
in the night
footsteps
heard
footsteps
a series
footsteps

occurring
long after
the event
occurred

hearing metal
is your horizon
in the night
not the word's late echo
not 'afterwards'
or 'meaningful'

i had already seen burning metal
during the day and thought it was the
twisted metal of a plane i had seen

my self lying face down in the river i
had seen a dead man lying in the
street and a small crowd looking at
him after him precious life

the sequence could be
'tropical night'
the nausea
has
no se-
quence

is the act
of its
occurring

does he want
his death seen
as he wakes up
in the bunk
in the trembling ship
to his death

wants a person
to die his death

i cannot do it

it is my own death

i am dying
and cannot die

asphyxial
asphyxiated
completely fucked
abominations & effects

the ship shakes gently on the way
home from the Japanese prison camp
and also then burning metal orange
flames a blue colour also suffocates or
you reach the sea and drown nausea
saturates again no body one single
sickness again he demands a witness
to his death the exact moment again i
am not able to do it later heavy
gasping breath of men dying many
deaths later in the night breathing
like a lover in the night

hwat is there to be done?

is
absolute love

not to be
in language
no

it’s a scar

no

the mark, the law

no

hhhhwat

is to be done?

second materialist exercise

i) the event occurs long after it occurred

ii) in dead time there's no event

iii) in dead time pain and sorrow cannot be purged

iv) in deathless desire there are zombies or there's revolution

iv) in resurrection no god no angels

'bullshit jobs'

1.
the moral and spiritual damage that
comes from this situation is profound.
it is a scar across our collective soul.
yet virtually no-one talks about it
(David Graeber you wrote that

there is no collective soul
the only thing that is is a wound
where can it be written

2.
the horrible shine
not-sun

you extract some speech
designating 'our soul'

self-murder

what's really missing

3.
pigeons
make a circle
aren’t there
which is for the human

something’s missing

wind
seagulls from brighton
hissing of leaves

(6 times

((66 times

4.
working time
working work
working not working
working death
the factory is everywhere

first materialist exercise

i) no page   no book   black square

ii) what are you going to do

iii) what they are doing   is history   no

iv) the law   is suspended   what are you going to do

I look at the dark leaves

i look at the dark leaves
then the green ones
memory
if it is
some memories
i look at the dark leaves
then the other ones
there's no relation
between them
zero in common
what they have in common
is zero

concrete railings spikes barbed wire

railings concrete metal people-barriers

miro las hojas oscuras
después las verdes
la memoria
si es
algunas memorias
miro las hojas oscuras
después las otras
no hay relación
entre ellas
cero en común
lo que tienen en común
es cero

concreto rejas pinchos
alambre de púa
rejas concreto barreras
de control metálicas

Translation by Ricardo Cázares

Letter to Timothy Garton Ash

For Stephen Watts

have you walked from Blackfriars to the
Strand through the legal gardens and
smelt the death molecules in the air
not the infectious miasma of bodies that
threatened to close everything down
including the novel itself in Dickens's
Bleak House   because European
social democracy has cleaned up and
removed it it also removed anything
that could have stopped fascism that's
not part of your narrative   the last
palace of words   the body as it denies
it

we shall never serve
under a red flag
the magic word
and black reflux after
Athens and Schäuble
and the will of the people
trodden and pissed on
(to make sure they won't do it again)

reduced to particles anxiety
hunted burnt or gassed
imprisoned at
what has no name

have you felt the death molecules in the air
the particles that penetrate your words
can you hear the
time alarm
when the dead demand
the food they didn't eat
which Ritsos heard in the Makrónisos prison
Greek Civil War 1949
European social democracy

Putin must be stopped and sometimes
only guns can stop guns
Schäuble is one of the most remarkable
politicians I have known
at the end of the day what matters is what will work
yes you wrote that

but schäuble is actually insane and
it's the voice of the dead says it
and can you hear it

hunted burnt and gassed

the unvomited

vomit vomit vomit vomit vomit vomit vomit

pain
name

the place has no
name
is not a place

say syria, palestine, hungary, germany, england and others
say it's easier to destroy the world
than to destroy capitalism
capitalism

say black square
is the place

in which
dead do walk

overlapping
not overlapping

Thatcher's dead

on the way to the party on the 159 did you
know that Jimmy Savile was a friend of
Thatcher's and what about all the other child
molesters but Rolf Harris wasn't was he i was
fined 80 quid for pissing in the street did you
know if a pregnant woman wants to piss a
policeman is obliged to hold up his cape and
protect her the one who said that was
probably a cop SWP he said

inside a crime
is where i'm going

Margaret Thatcher died today
long live death i shouted
that's a fascist slogan you said
it's ours today i said
viva la muerte

her bag of bleeding flesh
and the cynical morning
and the murderous sky
let the music vomit her out

it would be better if you lined them up

against a wall and shot them than this grinding

i would not wish death on anyone
you said

i don’t desire to break her law
i want to have done with it
viva la muerte

I look at the trees (Wakehurst august 2015)

For Helen

i look at the trees vast and
magnificent……………………is not what i
want to say.

time does not pardon, Marcelino says who
has just seen two funerals of men younger
than himself. and the problem is you can't
say goodbye. half an hour later we see a huge
carp with a glittering back sliding slowly
through the brown water. the fish turns and
swims away. se fue sin despedirse. he went
without saying goodbye. and this is (just
(actually (precisely not what i want to say.

i look up at the leaves. they shimmer stiffly in
warm light and air. there is something else
there. mysterious, if you like. not
represented. this is not what i want to say.

there is something outside the figure of the
visible but accessible only through it. it is not
accessible. and this is not what i want to say.

the leaves move in the light are light there's
nothing here
that's not here.

i am an old man. nothing satisfies me.
i am not an old man.

an explosion heard in sleep last night. bombs
in athens.

except the voices of the dead.

'schäuble is actually insane'.

for Ioulia

ferryman
(coin for him in your mouth

the redness of it

or you can put it on your forehead
with a headband
like Antigone did
for herself
and her brother

her wildly screaming

the spirit of ever-living and unwritten wilderness
and of the world of the dead – Hölderlin, 'Antigone'.

her wild tears
at dawn
cut the knot of pleasure
with total scission

someone else is the witness
there is no witness
spectres turn away

ah corpse-eaters
and murderers of the dead
oh tories and labour and corporations and hedge funds and IMF and
ECB and EU finance ministers
and all you who shit on the poor the disabled the out of work the
non-bullies the exploited in bullshit jobs
the unnecessary
you're the dead dead

the immortal dead
wait for justice

no more suicides!

thanatorium

this place
is a thanatorium
which means an establishment
where people are received
in order to die or be killed
(i have organised their death)

interference analysis
threat imaging
solution for objects
armour mobility
high security
perimeter protection
(for us)

or any other type
of death procedure

white maggots
hidden from daylight
munch our flesh

the maggots are imaginary and white
and they express what's invisible
it makes no difference

wind on the hills
what hills

horrible
in mediocre feebleness of time

when the sun-wheel turns
the spit of love
it is not all

why did you write about that

i had been thinking of writing a narrative, about a 12 year old boy who kills his mother on his birthday. the entire tomb of his birthday. maybe a prison diary.

there is no relation between the objects in the bedroom – an old wash-stand without a basin, a plain chest of drawers just big enough for his clothes, an old bed with a sagging metal mesh instead of springs, and to the left of the bed a chaos of things once of interest and now going dusty. gone into dusty.

there is no connection between the events of the day. vortex of dead regimes.

the sleep that follows murder is not sleep you are eternally awake.

guilt depends upon homogeneous empty time. in the parable of the vineyard-owner there is no accumulation of debt or of time. present-time bursts out of the dust of class society. you weep. your longing solders joy and sorrow. a convulsion of your body. a small piece of death.

i asked myself, before sleeping, what is it i want most from love. in a waking dream I am already inside the thing I want to understand.

it was the wrong question. faithless. i am looking for the influence of something on something when they are already interwoven. i am already interwoven.

the careless message that forms itself out of silence.

seconds through the rain, the air. there is no cosmos.

the landscape, has been destroyed.

i wake up, screaming in the night. i am submerged and cannot emerge. waking and sleeping have swapped places. i am conscious and can't wake up. before sleeping i was making a calculation so as to come to a decision.

it's in the vast emptiness that love occurs, not in the familiar.

a common place

for Robert Sheppard

and what is
by an immense subjective force
the common place
una bóveda incalculable
under grammatical skin
the anti-poem
because the coming body is female
(inconsistent with what you are)
is a fourth body
(like some flesh)
in fact tenderness
(keeping it and losing it)

like the god cannot extricate himself
the place of the heart destroyed

oh god
oh scorpion
who drags a bone
on what track what surface?

the gas of fear

the disabled suicided jobless and
workers abjected

'it is wrong'

during the news
action is only memory
i have no memory
is excess or visible stumbling-block
eyes would
stand
in opaque word
something got stuck there
(hurt)
the practical present

a wild mackandering shout
against slavery
against destitution
in syntagma square
from Mackandal
who was burnt and resurrected
in Sainte Domingue (which is Haiti now) in 1758

against slavery
which is debt slavery and work slavery
of most humans
who are not managers or capitalists

the non-present of present time
fast breeder

total secrecy
financial interests

the consolation of   actually living
                                      communism
not   tomorrow
not
                                      its impossibility

in data of impossibility

is not sleeping   (count
the light as dawn   (coming over the city   (as-light

obviously   obviously
extremetenderness

‘it is wrong’
said the Tory Minister for Modern Slavery

that there should be ethics
the body cut across by love
(cannot be

no body cut across by dawn light
no one cut across by love
it cannot occur

The slave Mackandal, a houngan knowledgeable of poisons, organized a widespread plot to poison the masters, their water supplies and animals. The movement spread great terror among the slave owners and killed hundreds before the secret of Mackandal was tortured from a slave.

a new face of death in german society

dead body and
describes
routine algebra
extracting space
north winds etc

mops up
the first useless Sunday dawning of the corpses
spirit dead
we use the acoustic noun
deathless desire
shafted by sunlight
on a day in july
in which space is
every sound
in praise of lust
swims through the honey
across the city of shit

do you know
your location

you cannot now not

fifth materialist exercise

i) reorganize the body with training   with consequences

ii) or resign yourself

iii) you can wake up as much as you like

iv) without rebellion   there's no real time

extracted

i am with my mother visiting some people a social
visit social unit having tea some tea the person
opposite is feeding off me off of cake a tall man
false man i am giving him substance I am giving
him of my substance out of a vertical wound in my
lower belly a large cut on the front of my stomach
which is a large vagina with lips which are lips
through which your substance is extracted

the man is boris johnson

Sixth materialist exercise

i) pure affect exists at a threshold   it's not yet tenderness

ii) at a threshold you can move 2 ways   it's a decision   sometimes presenting itself long after the event occurred

iii) the decision of love is against ideology   there is no suture

pickled

For Luna

i want to be
pickled like
they pickled enemies
alive
in the Wars of the Roses
in a big plastic sack
transparent polythene
and catapulted from Brixton or Tottenham
just where
a young black man was killed by the police
thrown by a huge trebuchet
through the air
until my pickled
body crashes through the roof
of that thing called parliament
and lands on that table
where the political dolls
play the games of capital
which have mucked
the full shining moon
at that point it's obvious what happens
the concentrated stink of debt
bursts out of my shattered body
which is compounded of
condensed bodies

a whole debtors' prison
poisoning the air
the parliamentarians swoon
as they breathe the noxious
gasses and start to choke
one by one

blanket off

one
                    one
pull blanket off
off
who
is
who
are you

one
some   one
big one
at trying to get
into my bed
¿quién eres?

hands
come
blanket off

apparitions

whose invading hand
whose breath
breathed by a

iron lung
does it
love me
can it say
it not

huge apparatus
no marks on the
dolly belly

ideology = phenomenology

a man is
dying on the floor
of a plane
at heathrow
can't breathe
restrained by
security guards
passengers don't
get out of your seats
stewardesses
no
intervention
remembers
if it will remember
the death image
inside your
front door

non-fraternal
social being being
they are persuaded they are seeing

ýýýýý

the dying
will be

screamed
into general existence
or will
kill us

third materialist exercise

i) from the perspective of the last judgment   it will never come

ii) transpierced   act

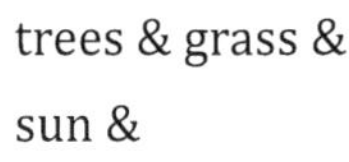

start the civil war

trees & grass &
sun &

something's been
disappeared

think with the whole body
what is the i-body

wanting a word
so it can forget

all banned subjects
banned by law

perfect body
is subjection gleams

body awaiting
some perversion

rub my belly
down

sun yellow and red and
down

won't bring being
face to face with itself

as capital says
abandon all hope
death's head descending
property & property & property

a horrible gleam
houses lawns cars eyes words children

validation of hate
= courage

revenge morning
against the arrow of time

weeping backwards tears backwards
validation of hate

herald of antigone brother
ayawaska sister

destruction and riot
= maximum intensity

produce
void

against prostitution of time
by Tory corporalities

fascinated by cruel
immortality of money

fascisted by the gleam
of that obedience

enjoy & enjoy & enjoy
smile up their arse

glue it all together
with sex

your production of time
tory voters

will today which is beautiful
tear us apart

destroy your pleasure
with absolute rending of appearance

formerly called
apocalypse

start the civil war

messiah

but then he dies
that was like thirsty
like thinking
self-spitting
before pills
in the bedroom
and falls back into

the non-dream
stubborn
like some   interval thing
can it   or does it

River Effra

river effra
effroi
euphrates
oh brothers
i mean / all the
names were / (said fraternally

walk on the river
What's your name
ese día me suicido
yes what's your

ecstasy
nothing

for many days
i've been walking the sewer

(fuck my life
who?
manwomanish
erikryptos
completely hidden

not numerable

cut to MI6 / Vauxhall
eye
drain

the extreme head of ideology

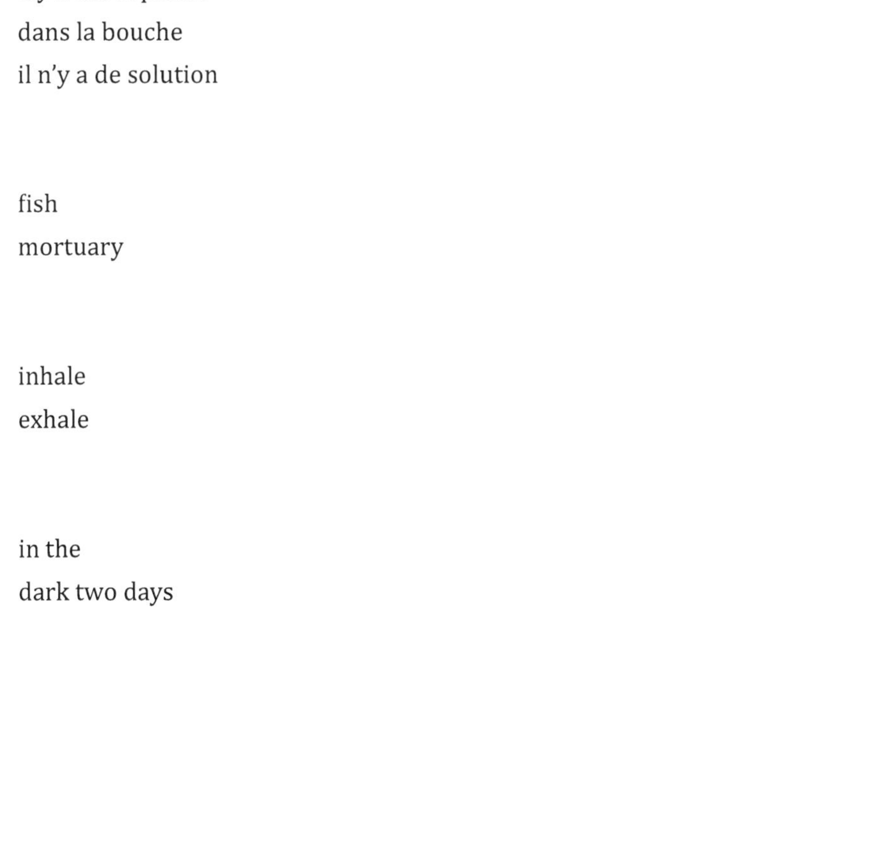

even if you killed him

afternoon

il y a des liquides
dans la bouche
il n'y a de solution

fish
mortuary

inhale
exhale

in the
dark two days

the absolute book

the cat could not be more
                              ////than its legs

were dying

bothered by shadows
                                        in the air

noise and incisions
of another
book

where something else////

makes four slashes
against the absolute heart

paths of lightning

a necessary collided form

spatial modification programmes
confirm as solitary our security
in the temporal metal
property screaming
reduced to minimal appearance
in what is not time
deadmen
come out of a wall

pornography
is what makes your poetry cohere

space can
produce new worlds

yellow

yellow
some sort of
nowhere
some
yellow

red-yelow
places
if i could

see
with insect eye
i would

yellow
was-yellow
not yet

a written place

there are no words or sun
on my extended paper

so you are death
integument   rind
another   another

walls into white landscape

return to
some
/thoughts/
some
major violent systems

fourth materialist exercise

i) in comfort zones of death

ii) in continuity what terror

iii) in zones of delight what new worlds

skull on my bone

skull on my brain
bone and bone
tender and
just now wept

of which nature is only a part

found her
normal bones

does anything envelop anything

i am going to show how the place tilts

you need to know there is incessant division

dust
disrelated distressful
this need

my always time meadow

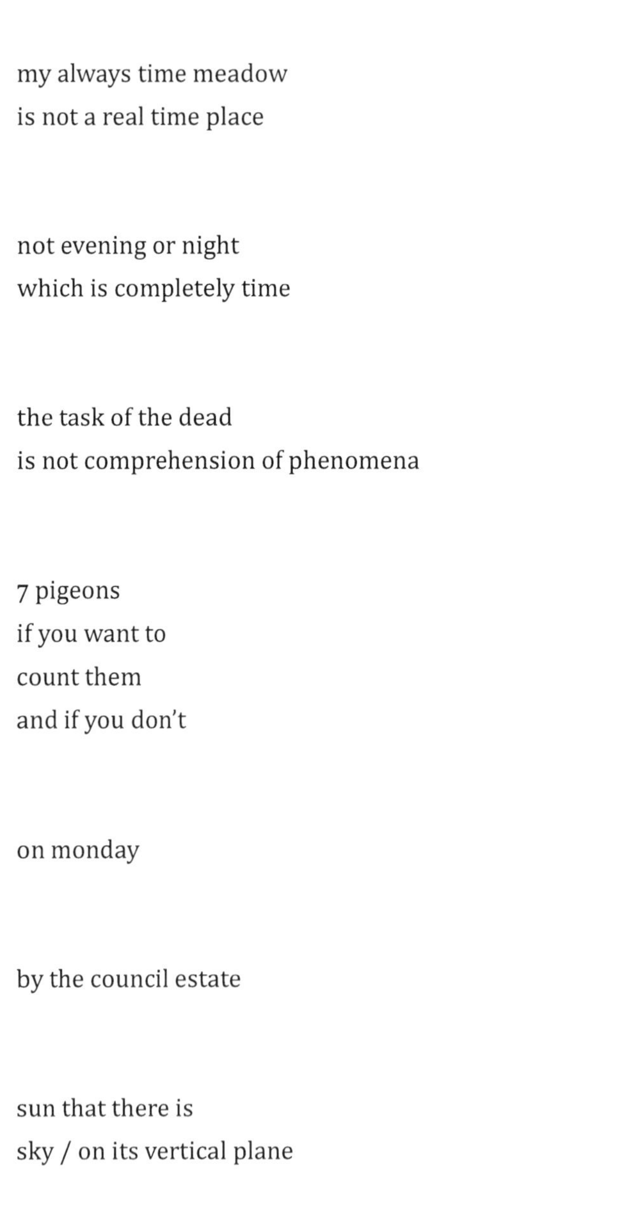

my always time meadow
is not a real time place

not evening or night
which is completely time

the task of the dead
is not comprehension of phenomena

7 pigeons
if you want to
count them
and if you don't

on monday

by the council estate

sun that there is
sky / on its vertical plane

destitute

without destitution

comes a void
the dead inhabit

where is the past that is a house

the sky
equated with the sun
has only one side

canary wharf 2

an event for which there's no image – Rilke

the same thing happened to them
when they lost their gherkin etc.
i'm talking about trainers were the
thing everyone wanted in the riots
remove the fetish and the whole
system collapses canary wharf on
fire

how memory has tarmacked and
concreted the place where i lived
removed space from it even the
pain which is the only thing you
take with you to the other side
trainers the thing the gherkin etc.

the perfume is macular the pain
has gone ni siquiera su espanto
está not even a spectre falluja it

brags loss of code it brags code and
you say how could Blair have lied

the manager's everywhere he's
getting fat the same thing
happened to them wind of other
planets wind of this

june 2015

the long body is tumbling
through these spaces
one segment
is missing

drunk on the jasmine at your door
graces
hurry hurry
to the world of the living

sometime
the rustle of all grass
in a field
fills the wound
of that conception
is the audible sound
in the left ear
a whistling bone
let it speak
but half-way round
its scission
when the spirit is once in command
or the spirit

INCISIONS (2014)

every point
belongs to
granular
parallelogram of
exquisite
pain which an-
aesthetic word cannot
not
every cosmic
entity
falls
out of
reference
it's addressing
your organic conforming
illusion
first note
pianissimo
painful already
in the interval of
between death
and slavery
its blood
they want
our
undreamed-of
solidarity
brothers and sisters
what's

between
them and
us
nothing
but a colourless
vacant space
to wake up
to
edges
have nothing
between
i think
nothing's
going to happen
in this country
it's
never
going
to stop
i get rid of the people
& i keep the money
i uncouple them
& i blindfold &
lock them out of it
this is the best part
give me
more
an insect
a breeze
words hacking
against their silence
has
anxiety
word
by word

there's an urgency
or necessity
in these poems
that isn't bound
by or even
especially
references
desire
lots of people
have moved out
since this benefit
came into effect
and
suffering's
the
word
the next instrument
is a violent instrument
the next steady state
is generalised bullying
John Locke
Strategy Fund
Class 1 Shares
EJLIX
something's not there
abstract labour
abattoir
see how it's censored completely
in unanimous metals
a clear narrative of British progress
with proper emphasis on heroes and heroines
a bottle of formol
in which dead things may be seen
the anima soul
but how it was never

completely immersed
like i am
completely immersed
or was it
in my body
completely
how many dead bodies inside your £6 billion
blood fest
pure culture breathing
albatross
unsmudged
i think it gives me anxiety
which in your vomiting is music
completely
submit
to
yellow
the
political
is
dis-
agreement
as
to
what
reality is
and then what
how to spend it
well black
toilet paper
were they
ever themselves
since they were not
born
is

hunger
in the
night
a woman's life
has
its mirror
god's
in his word
seeds
to do the
die in
no
not *my* pain
but everyone's
no
not *everyone's*
but the one that
is the
commune
like corralled by colours
and /obviously/ attacked by numbers
because you can't move
because your body is made of mirrors
they reflect
suffering
from any number of distinct places
just such a composition
it can't be fair for people
who have no right to be in the UK
to continue
to exist
as
everybody
else does
May said

wake up to
vacant space and
is there an image
somewhere else
my body
somewhere in my body
standing up
or down
the place wasn't there
the signs don't correspond
to the earth
does the earth
we rub our bodies together
and laugh out loud
skin to skin
is that a place
the city according to the senses
walking through control areas
suicides of disabled people
one after another
emerge from some slight billowing clouds
condensed
white
falling in that vacant place
wreckage of the clinging body
it is the
wreckage you are
going into
rewiring infinity
to reconciliation
with the enemy
no!
goes and offers me the corpse of time
well & that's not melancholy enough
offers me the fake end of time

the fake
journey we all make
from birth (I wasn't there
to death
(not there either
the dead marched on London
it was like one cemetery
after another and
another in the same place
making a lamentation
between the lungs
and the stomach the earth
will never close over
I see strips of a suffering & a
microbe sickness
germinating
grieving
tender
fierce
spewing
so much
giving me
to vomit
me given to vomit
forever language matter grief
almost everything
an owl
has ripped up
my poems
brightness   in your eyes
so bright
bitterness
if he is you   in you
carry him
on your back

or in
your stomach
got no sense
no *mouth*
saw a lot of vegetables
what have they done to you?
if there's a chain
of abjects
not pain
of association

pain
as in a lake
but a lake
is useless
I need
to know
what the word
is not
put the meaning back
in words
take
food from supermarkets
this is crime
whose name
is done
to us
what is it allows
your poetry
to make sense
when it shouldn't
make sense at all

what medicine prevents
me being sick
I want to vomit it up
doctor dog
the Requirement
is to
submit to
IDS
who represents
the British state
which represents
the Pyramids of Egypt
a completely mirrored sexbox
which represents movement
entertaining
the species
while numbers
burn
somewhere else
the furor of poetry
unattachable appearance
like flies
in the wind
the earth
could be
here
and
paradise
i felt happy
to see
my world
as pictures
choking
blood-blinded
i woke up to

language
inside the court
it's like being in love
with property
when you get out
the street
it
gleams
less
the memory asleep
in the memory
museum
the workers
asleep in the
con-
crete
outside
an acoustic
surge
in the eye-
ball
a non-
word
in the langua-
ge
the nightingale
heard at 2.30 am
by Freer, McCardle and Rowe
for 20 minutes or so
after a reading in Berlin
was Bob
full-throated ease
not one phrase repeated
red creeper is
dark rust red

virginia creeper
you said
joyous and
equal
to
violence
i see words
in the air
calling
to
their
being
there

pain is not in your words but
somewhere else
afterwards
grieving
among the rats
violent non-violent
what it's like
to be poor
it's not just that they
it's not just that they are cruel
(they are cruel)
do not be afraid to say what they do
is terror
is low intensity low
terror
which
doesn't make it less
than

high
intensity
terror
duration
the
duration
inside
is terrible
the point is
how to get outside
you may say
but there isn't one

a silken thread
part of the unravelling
colour
of love
the fragility
of light
is this and
in this area
that cannot see
part of the light
turned back
by the lexicon
of the sun
object that gimmers
back
ok glimmers
but in our system
in our shadows
without which

there would be none
or less than none

shitless
stutters
trembling like a leaf
the pages of the book
are absolutely white
the last few shadows
of letters   erased
disappear
i have lived
i am here
individual
trans-individual (pronoun dead)
faithful territory
psychic territory
in this order
let that explain

modifying genes could
give us a longer
life-span
greater intelligence
ability to breathe
poisonous atmospheres
a true diaspora of life
that would have started
with us

as we cross
interstellar space
we will unlock
nature's greatest
secrets
why the universe
existed at all
we are only the temporary
custodians
of the particles we are made of
the universe bonds with me

dizzy like
2 sides
never
off of each other
but in 'mind'
what follows
modifies
mediates
nowhere
for a perfect
sleep
I tried to
find it
nowhere
all
the desert and the desert
that Tory come
all over me
I wipe it off
but there's

more
learn
to
swim
in the convex
spoon
particles
swarm and shake
with Brownian
movement
is this a cause
for hope
upright tilt
think
the sun
has come
out
and the leaves
throbbing in the
air
another
doll's house
in the rapid eye
in San Francisco the spectres shine
i stare at the edge
is this a curse
all-positive
you-assembly
emotion
during the days of everything
carnivorous aggression
seemed to be the mystery of days
ecstatic heat
in the bodies of gods
the supreme concept of bourgeois society

the concept of police
I need 10,000 pills
to get to the next place
no
once again I will write the book
of agitation
swerving all the time
no more
burial remedies

LAW (2013)

Law: Andalucía

They took some food from a
supermarket to give to people
who needed it. Robbery.
Suspended sentence. Two years.
And not go within 200 metres of
the supermarket. And not go
within 100 metres of the
checkout woman who cried.

Law: The London Legacy Development Corporation

vast new areas of
new open space

an atmosphere of trust and neighbourliness
and a village
atmosphere

one of the delights
of the legacy
is this whole
event
will be giving back
a park to East London

the green and pleasant
land still
exists

negligence
ecstasy

Law: scansion

lit the olympic torch i
says Boris Johnson i
love the smell of legacy in the morning

lost their temple
lost their revenge
all over again

Law: London Olympics

they give you a asbo
they give you a park
where kissing is prohibited

they give you missiles to protect you in the air
soldiers on the streets
more than in Afghanistan

the largest security op since the 2nd world war
they say it's going to be a victorious summer
they say believe in britain

it's high intensity private ownership
of everything
it's a sponsored security show
                                        anxiety show

god save the queen
and god save god from the multitude
queen from the slobbering crowd

it's everyone's london 2012
everyone's pspo

Law: Stratford is not a hallucination, Iain Sinclair is wrong

he's fucking he's fucking he's fucking
he's fucking
you

as if any Christ scythed through nature
will be your bliss

your
come
undead desire

missiles camp
and jerk and relate
dense layers of financialised risk

grindr and i
bring the event
closer to
you

if you don't enjoy
there's something

wrong with
you

with YOU

law: discipline permits intelligent violence

'protesters have acted
with remarkable
discipline and restraint'

this is
a people
robbed and spoken
is the saying of it

you ingratiate
contrapersons
at the exact-point

where courage is lost
i move war
through your sentiments

we are the lords of time
the jagged line
the void

Law: it was sadder than money

i will make a book

of horrible silence

it emerges out of noise

how syllables affect the living

within the concave of the phrase

i am well connected

Eton laughter

Law: depression

the insect isn't there
ate his way out of the apple
unlike the one
i woke up
at breakfast
squashed

dirty tracks

the one is all things
the other a hole

the insects and the apple say nothing

Law: sentences

i will enjoy
like 4 times you did it

love to me
so what

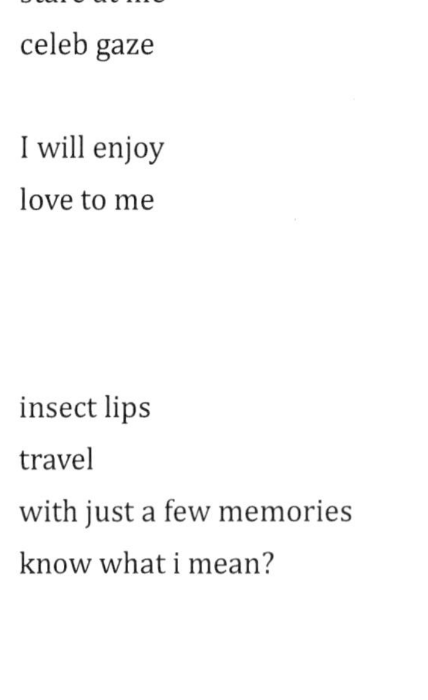

stare at me
celeb gaze

I will enjoy
love to me

insect lips
travel
with just a few memories
know what i mean?

insect lips
divine
mine

Law: name

but it’s doing something else
    the rain’s
        doing something else
            like helicopters

like syllables of
    names
        coming down

normal skin and
    normal hair
        care

Law: considering the forms of thought

so long as my blood is attached
to the world I live for by its motion
– Keston Sutherland

the blood circulates
attaches no one
to any one

in that respect
is
similar to capital

continues into
what goddam future?

Law: immense labour

immense labour
of the homeless person-woman-man-child
furrows the planet

because our having nothing
is images of utter change
as for perceiving

we think straight
it's already too late
the lack of exodic music

is the law
walking from Mali
to the Mediterranean

saw many die
on the way

Law: murder

country supper
and other charms of state
owe you so much
renewing the tie
to the land

unrepresented

our murder sleeps

Law: the State

this one is all the things he dreams of
the other a body in space
homeless

you don't know what the State is capable of

Law: benefits (what the government told nicky melville)

we cannot pay you
because you have
as much or more money
coming in than
the law says
you need to live on

Law: notrecht

the law had vomited them out
ask the pope else

he kisses the feet
of prisoners

like meat
the series I had
fallen through the gas

that we should leave them there
like iraq
nobody was there

Law: maths

Refute objects!
syntax   gang
with convulsive writing
dilates the pupils
on both sides of the law
with something strictly uncountable
pain in mathematics

THE SPECTRE (2013)

the spectre

for Ulli Freer

how i vomit
vomit enough
how i do do it
and i want to do it

very much faster
than they present themselves

ungoverned spaces and
security vacuum

the horsemeat
in the english language
if i put it
in my mouth

shine

soho
6.30pm

raindrops
on a black BMW

the streets
are reconciled

grand

the only thing about
our epoch that could
be called grand is
the revolution that shadows
it the revolution it
failed to carry out

sacrifice is our nexus
a sex machine
that extends to the sun

extreme wishes

walked
hundreds of thousands
of streets
without passion
with passion
the object never changes
something's always happening
it's supposed to be now
it's as stiff as
eight edges
of sheer noise
it's extreme wishes of the dead
to kill
the jerking perverts
of capital
fuck me
like an animal

homage to the Popol Wuj

esquirlas
splinters
la dura dura realidad

somos las madres
somos los padres
de las palabras

no

absolute despair
squamous carcinoma

its' a decision
on a body

rage
be violent
you're already dead

NO

ALL HUMANS ARE EQUAL
let that be violent

face

in the ruin of my vocabulary
some thing
mutilation happened
i started to write
some deeper catastrophe

then men with secrets
came
a chemise
a dream
in mother

9 men rape
with faces
i was
happened on my birthday

i
stroke a horse
immersed in himself
the face
is on your face
the face is on my face

never the name

a mouthful of biscuit
all the sorrow

the bones cry out

no

there were
phrases
without words

the form of trees in winter
          (bare branches   wind

swirls of
leaves
never the same
                    never
the name

someone for whom there are
no words
          gave the measure
  (or could not find it

my perfection, said Descartes

enough pain for several lives

leaves
dust
swirls
in swirls

for whom

i
wasn’t there

the dark end of it
and the storm
is standing on your head

is nothing but a shroud of time

it only comes to be
by being left behind

a mouthful of wind

in the dead newborn throat

billionaire

he wants
a number
big enough
to do the job
of Buddha

SPIT SPIT & SPIT

human needs
& not
debt
=
wealth
so

START AGAIN

animal cage

trapped in the animal cage
the first cock his mattin rings

rage

this is the creature that wasn't born
horn

this blue baby's
already an old man
he coughs and worries you
and looks out of his eyes
with the death of the species

rain comes down
on the hospital

this availability of death

for Geraldine

blue again
and brown and black and yellow
and the paths (of sound

scratching a path
sparrows'
feet on

the toast
outside the window
already

why didn't you
smell it burning
grand appreciation

the waxy
blue flowers
you did

didn't you
in the creaky
old toaster

sparrow toes
scratch? climb?
walk? turn?

turn up the

blue hydrangea
a chalky blue

peculiar clotted noise
clumsy first cigarette
of the day

again
why didn't you
notice

the path of sound
feet in the air
breathing

where
did you
get so cheeky

you did
didn't you
and heard the whisky

and the three
ships sailing
by

helpful banking

For Nick e Melville

switch
to a more helpful bank

help me to die

Canary Wharf 1

money
on the walls

how the money fell out
when we rioted

why should anybody know
what that is

hear the wind
speak cash

ah Hegel
the absolute flux of appearances

the song of sleeping somewhere is
croaking raven
hear a human's death

when you hear words full
of the things themselves
ask how

shakespeare in love
and everyone seems to believe it
if they are humans

how legal is it

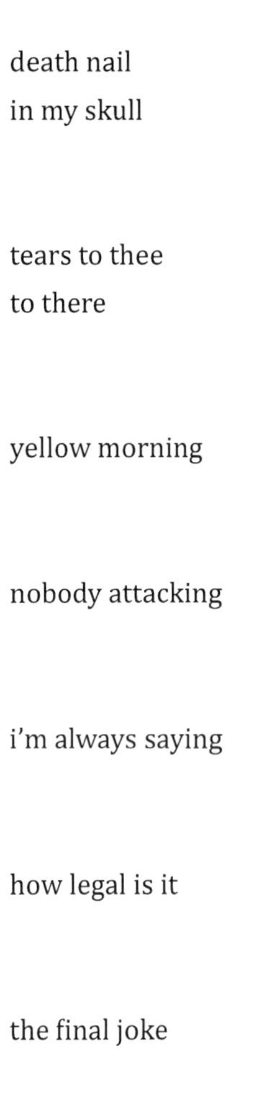

death nail
in my skull

tears to thee
to there

yellow morning

nobody attacking

i'm always saying

how legal is it

the final joke

plug hole

the world can be understood
as an idea

the world can
not be understood
as an idea

where it blows

the first man who began
to speak
whoever he was
must have included it

aftermouth

time

DEATH ON THE NHS

UNNECESSARY DEATH IS WALKING AMONG US
HE'S A FRIEND OF THE TORIES

HE'S STALKING YOUR HOSPITAL NOW
AND HE'S A FRIEND OF THE TORIES

SLEEP SOFTLY IN MY ARMS, SAYS DEATH
HE'S A FRIEND OF THE TORIES

GIVE ME YOUR HAND, SAYS DEATH
WHEN YOU LIE IN THE GUTTER

YOUR GUTS ARE MINE, SAYS DEATH
AND HE'S A FRIEND OF THE TORIES

OH BONES, DO NOT CRY OUT, SAYS DEATH,
PEOPLE MIGHT HEAR YOU
YOU'RE NO FRIEND OF THE TORIES

memory of future happiness

what
was it
massing in the trees
between evening and night
on Walton Heath
the interior dream
of your system eyes
a shimmering substance
beside itself
on the golf course
a theory of value
from which it is not possible
to subtract yourself

NATION (2012/2015)

the sound of pigs falling

the sound of pigs falling
has fallen out of words
///dear dead///
some next-level revolution coming
cancels your silence
punching holes in the name of things
which body
from our bodies fall
the people armed
never be
mystical dreams
in other words
exceeds
its representation
poetry is a virus
mutating
right
in front
of your face

nation

they find nostalgia, they find heritage, in the nation state
– Sir Simon Jenkins

thought stop money thought some
money thought money

some money thought money

thought money thought

the gass
passes through

fiery green
day breaks
what utopia

the stars grim on their black stalks
all of them polar opposites is
corporate synthesis

impunity
layer upon layer

is our alphabet
dead radio voices
in the sun

I am seeing something else
irrefutable insect survival
secret endless food

it's empty mate

the body is
being dead
had fallen out of words

lack of courage is
stopping me from writing

I am flayed
with water and sparrows

I walk away from a university
with a delayed dictionary

sterile zone
peripheral buffer

it's the year
of the Olympics

index

there's someone
whose need is reversed

the air is full
of the cries of men and women
signals
expunged unexpunged

the air is his book

chained to the morning
already cast early sky ribs
the same thing rising

nothing is missing

Carpetright

Post Office

Boots

JD Sports

O2

Currys

Argos

PC World

Comet

H&M

HMV

Haringey Magistrate's Court

Haringey Shopping Centre

Gay's the Word

Aldi

H&M

JD Sports

Fire engine

Fire engine

Carphone Warehouse

T-Mobile

Design Studio

Fire engine

JD Sports

Argos

MacDonalds

W H Smith

Blockbuster

Tesco

Tottenham Hotspur Football Club

Kelmscott Secondary School

Dalston Kingsland Centre

Bus and police cars

Foot Locker

Halfords

Currys
Police car
Sainsbury's
Police car
Valens Jewellers
Ozcam Jewellers
JD Sports
Sainsbury's
Savers
Foot Locker
Carphone Warehouse
Evans Cycles
Jamie's Italian
Currys
Halfords
Brazas Restaurant
National Express bus
Sony Distribution Centre
Palisades Shopping Centre
Bullring Shopping Centre
Pure Gym
Tesco
Addidas
Ealing Broadway Station
Tottenham Centre Retail Park
Jessops
Game
Police car
JD Sports
Argos
Harveys
Mothercare
JD Sports
Debenhams
Burger King

Ladbrokes

Bus

Argos

Betfred

Sainsbury's

Topshop

Argos

O2

Carphone Warehouse

Phone 4U

Cash Converters

Foot Locker

Boots

Barclays

The Ledbury

MacDonalds

Reading Angling Centre

Greggs

Cyber Candy

Richer sounds

Money Shop

Diesel

Bang & Olafsen

Swarovski

Tesco Express

Bromley South Station

Argos

Primark

Arndale Centre

Foot Asylum

Bargain Booze

Miss Selfridge

Square Peg Pub

Orange

Reeves

T-Mobile
Austin Reed
Jessops
MacDonald's
Admiral Street Police Station
Tesco Express
Jamaica Inn
Thomas Sabo
Cabot Circus Shopping Centre
Gas main
Vodafone
Clarence Convenience Store
Clarks
Primark
H Pollock
Salford Shopping City
3 Mobile
Ugg
Meadows Police Station
Job Centre
Macro
Great Harry Pub
Coral
Sainsburys
Life
Canning Circus Police Station
Marks & Spencer
Orange
Patisserie Valerie
Kro Bar
Café Nero
Burton
Pretty Green
Picadilly Museums
Wimpy

Charles Dance Jewellers

No**1** Pizza

House of Fraser

JD Sports

Liver Launderette

Belal’s Newsagent

ASDA

ASDA

Bloc Inc

Jessops

something strictly unnamable
happens to the image of suffering
and what this has to do with riot
by previously existing criminals
political and final stone

learning to learn

learning
to hear
the dispute within the waves

Whitman too

could hear the stems
thrusting through the earth

but the line of fire in the street
still burning burns

utopian fire

feel the joy of appetite
in blood and fire

interrupt
the boundless azure

gaze of the rulers
all the pores of hatred open

pour a line of petrol on the street
it'll keep the police busy

death speaks ordinary language

death speaks ordinary language
civilisation stuff
what will be the fulcrum of my eyes?

how discover
political action
with the humans on our backs

I am accompanied by someone else
it needs to be
how to kill
written on the air

is there anywhere a force strong enough to put an end to this state of affairs? -

Hugo Ball

the walls of the cell
time hardens
demands a vast theatre
the person breaks out of life
fierce moments
innumerable rays
the situation
not coded or decoded / or opaque or transparent
the money signifier / is one of semblance
then find a better one
I am heading towards certain territories
hooliganed
it's December always
at the repair place

rough work

to grasp an opportunity in the
current abyss instead of
submitting to the wreck of our
common life by clinging to the
old meanings / what's to be done with

an apparition which has a left hand

a glue so simple it sticks memory to good intention with ideas of repair

it's the false beloved

a warm and mild apparition

like so many obsolete
compounds

like opinion

there is an absolute moment of
composition which grasps the
void of this situation

revolution

revolution anyway

the shopping mall is burning

the shopping mall is burning
end of my silence
my slot perspectives
scopic error
cream suck
non-conjunction and non-disjunction
infants used as signs
here are real repairs
sends the runner
something good appear
imagine reference from words
when to shift gaze
integrated discrete programme
time-shifted vocabulary of learning

there is nothing to do
there is only the effort to wake up
and the possibility you won't
it has already happened several times
before the person can think or know
who shehe is
the cloned
eyes go to sleep
is voices   and is not
new forms of barbarism
or general emancipation

found event

by entering the event
you give your express consent
for your actual or simulated likeness
to be included in any and all media
for any purpose at any time
this includes filming by the police

Stefan George

shadows of the sea
still surf
still sky
the pretense of the day

the bride wrapped in silence

chords of spray

voices calling

the dazzling crown of words

and
the militarization of space
has already happened

Soviet Factory

The Red Flag Textile Factory St Petersburg
Photographed by Richard Pare 1999
An image
of hope
(gone ((gone) (((lost
and did it smell like this then?

money

money

walking around

smell / washed out

orgasm and
other colours

the unground enters

a complex of hole agencies and obscure
surfaces unground the earth . . . once
freed from its solar slavery the
earth can rise against the Sun
and its solar capitalism

that we should be so lucky

the sun reddens

the sun reddens
it interdicts itself
the silence reddens

I am instructed

I am instructed in space and affect

to curse the event

the intense common light

dawn in dawn light

bad eye movement

incarceration

animalia

the language of the dice
the hot disease which I hear
turns
to exile
an appropriate obsessing technique
like natural
to the natural orifice
office

into her body they put you again
explicit monsters
they put you into your body again
syntax
gang
convulsive writing
dilates the
genitals
on the other slope
dice speak

illuminist

so many instruments
 dreamed
of a thing not
 dreamed
mud-coloured flesh
 I'm so glad so glad
it's the sound of human sound
 water breaking
all the beings that exist in the water will die
 hence the need for their illumination
produces rapid eye movement
 produces movement
cars burning in Paris suburbs
 conflagrations
exact calibrations of injustice
 it's the 20th of October
the frenzy of youth

thanks Jeff

what I was the   organ

what I want was

I want to be that thing

there is no explanation

loathsome familiarity

loathsome familiarity
of the sex partner
the interminable abyss
can't be said or removed either
the false evening
what it said

bundled

bundled
by wild yellow or gold
faster than word sounds
my reason for
turning away from them

outlived lives

what does it mean
to do the thing
which exceeds everything
for eternal purposes
drive through the actual gas
the outgoing screams
vacating something that's
even the frame
((even the furnace

spot the early signs of madness

spot the early signs of madness
keep the person a little bit longer
I'm not worried if you're not worried

if you're worried see your doctor
for symptoms caused by damage and loss

remember past events and problems
hard to follow tv programmes

spot the early
signs of your
dementia

the king's speech

he did learn to speak
but could not say
a single true word
even with the help
of Winston Churchill
and Simon Schama
and Rowan Williams
etc.

you are the gatekeeper

you are the gatekeeper
you are the interior trace of hunger
gaslight in a glass column
the inheritor, the tree
enjoyment of this society
as someone who has always died
will eternally be ripped off
by the corrupting demons of the air

Bill knocked out

his disgust
for disgust
his painunbound
departure for new affection and wound
the line refraction
of something that
if hell
speaks
prevents that thing from being seen
but the soft drill
of the poem
ah reader
the small swirl of letters
touches it
they
were of the party of death
dust and rain in the gutter
who can stop its arrow

condition of hope

the air in sunlight and beyond
the line that is waiting
a swerve away from them
during the colour of the sky
will always shine like clouds
a kiss away
from palaces of the real
always outside itself
we are 2 in evening
the complex lens
the evening at last
pale mauve or whisky
the strata of the air
after rain
indistinct
distinct

beyond desire another day

rich unattached rib
rises even in night
my previous contents
in the time place
exit into morning

'Bring back that black thing we did not have in our story'

the dusk leaves and shadows leave
light without shadow
no name
hallucinates them
1,700 drones
the wrong man
our thousand year plan
despair
air

frontal lobe

frontal lobe
is powerful new real and

lesion offer
cannot help us grasp it

being and shit

take part
share every human emotion

the actual screen
being luminous in the afternoon

the glow of capital

can you see it?

clock is natal sack

clock is natal sac
how you do do it
ruts in and in the river
always mirror mirror
yellow money
(how systems kill you
never worry)
always equilibrium
in the supreme presence
supreme police

the animal in the sawdust
kills time

slow acid

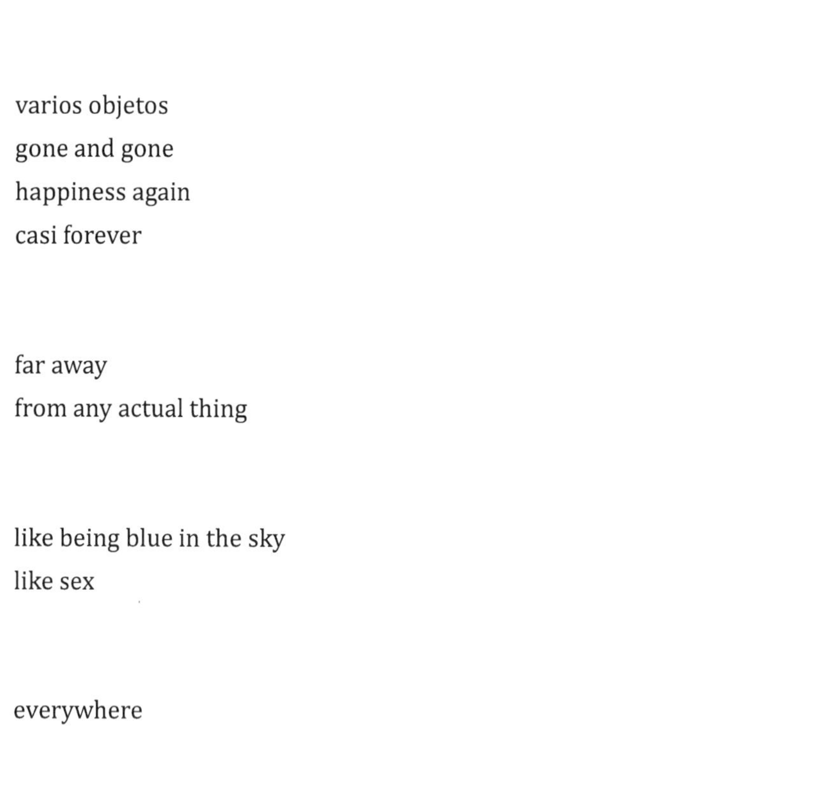

slow acid
ha!

it's the emotion
late dawn suicide

varios objetos
gone and gone
happiness again
casi forever

far away
from any actual thing

like being blue in the sky
like sex

everywhere

pale light flares

pale light flares
from the phenomenological plants
unfailing light
familiar music

too high a price

Royal Palace

royal apartments
royal medals
royals doing sport
royal toys
royal babies
princes doing sprache

abajo
la turbulencia incalculable de la lengua

always mesmerized by the parst

if i stayed in everlarsting time
i'd still have a little fuck

if we exit under money
the shit language hoovers life

our own
political thing

a gel of time

a gel of time
outer edge: saline

that man was in
the idea of myself
inside my bones

you have to be fearless
to put the beats
where he put them

turning up his red lamp
the years are stolen
there can be no negation
so that an old man may be born
silence become silence
the words closer

the real edge of fear is
'the real sound of the dead' (Spicer)
or are the wishes of the dead
for positive recognition
white and armless signals
seagulls?

now/awaken

now
awaken
into the head of the colonisers
put that in your frontal lobe
hellboy in your name to be
your frontal bone
make a curvature of
time against the
regime of
progress is oven
a social revolt
against the wind of time is blowing
murders
what your needs
actually are
brothers and sisters

you yourself a stranger

you yourself a stranger in that night
in the low glow of tv
resurrect the dead from winter
their mouths popping louder than names
faithful to you and not to any other
confidence in the ladder and not in the steps
in you and not in any other

hard as stone

for many days summer even in winter
the weird spine
the glow of that book
seen with this specter in its mouth
red segment
air of other wounds
ruining the mouth
without possible animal
what you do understand
so entirely without hope
ah gypsies
bitter yellow
don't trust the redeemers
where you do live the dead
continually and hissingly
the time fragment
related or unattended
music hard as stone

'plasm sac'

the white material
enters the lunacy period
the pigeons walk along the edges reading
the bought environment
the edges disappear

for Sean

There is a moment to each day that Satan cannot find
– Blake, *Milton*

strong psychic instru-
ment marks
chaos marks
political si-
lence penetra-
tes ruins of sound
where it dis-
appears
out of mind
that could
hold hell

'property makes us stupid'

what obscure
Courage what
Illumination how
blind could
see in
Property the
formless
and
reduced Beings
a memory
Gin repeatable
Theatre of
Wound less
than Violence
and more

subject to light

subject to light

the opium abstract

cancellation of luminous detail

song of the helicopter dawn

the slow segments of fury

promethean speed

materials necessary to produce the time

fallen out of systems

parts of themselves

suicidal time

the roar of that dimension

how out of life

how out of life
series too
is ripped out of series
tears from ----------------- disappeared
to --------------------------- disappeared

the wound says nothing
held the rudder
of that conception

the idea of
silence moving any faster

organised
in the
non-word

thought wants
to survive

you can only read the score
if you are death

more sacrificed women

A la sombra de los estucos
llegan viejos y zancos
en sus mamelucos
los vampiros blancos.

In the shadow of plastered
walls here come
in their suits
the long-legged white vampires.
– José María Eguren, 'La diosa ambarina' [The amber goddess]

what is mysterious
if the rain mocks and mocks
mocks and bellows

could the thing heard
not have known

if the word was
bootless volume

so the ones who die
without being born

there's a woman
buried
under each
single column

I am eight years old
every word hates hurts

more sacrificed women

on

sit in the
hospital it is
sitting for
something a
strong smell
already the
smell has
gone through
everything
this is the
stiff cuffs of
the nurses
and her cold
white hand
also the
brown walls
stiff white
virgins and
instruments
of your
present time
courage and
the lack of it
has passed
through all
the bodies
including the
father inside
the mother

and how it
might not be
this how we
might spit it
out lying on
a rubber
sheet and
how it might
grow into
you the thing
you choke
on

growth

the three black fans at the back of
some London buses which you can
see from the top deck of another
bus have a sinister look they seem
to be looking back at you
functionally if you think about it
rationally they must have to do
with ventilation in hot weather but
what is the function of the function
in november they weren't turning
though you could see the blades
were black in appearance they
indicate the fans of some larger
ducts like the ones that prevent a
factory combusting and killing the
workers what is the larger
machine for example the fans that
ventilate some of the tube tunnels
are much larger perhaps two or
three metres tall to blow enough air
so that passengers can breathe or
the fans you can see through the
intake of a jet engine at least two
metres high and think of the
quantity of air that is compressed
and pushed through them and the
wind that ventilates the city is it
enough the huge invisible fans the
ducts

POETRY EVERY DAY OF YOUR LIFE

the representation
of everyday life
is no different
from the representation
of dreams

in that case
how can we wake up?

viscera all over the city

plastic bullets kill

batons damage forever

their time is the administration
of death

WAKE UP!

THE EARTH HAS BEEN DESTROYED (2009)

Section 1

Another spell

in the
spliffed
eyes

a gaslake stood out

people were
hung
from hooks
in doorways

dead fingers
showed
out of
rubble

it was
promised

can you see to the other side

eyes craven in another spell

snitched
once in the garden w/ laughter

crawled like to the other

another
spell

Shameplace

Ah shameplace
and buyouterswound/dream
like spit in the eyes
like space

Or else
feldspray
darkwoven speechliness

Oh far off
oversucked
words

1:7:02

Sleep death poem

(final breath poem)

Rose glutton eye
gas gleam
cancer screen

shaft

wouldn't you

do the same?

Three in Brixton

a finger a shout
exploding dynamite story
negative genre
bound or otherwise
something like this
which I called Imagination

metaphors
which rush
back to a site
not maternity
click on the abstract
ways of handling hexameters
pre-reading
gleam of something harboured
water dispersible
parts of my body
lost all over the city

I suppose you can take this
now can't you
a rush of grace in the hands
a gothic run
all good lies could be substitutes

lost all tenacity

testicles they were
shoved
is he back tonight
I don't think I should have left him

laughs across gulfs
a good scrapbook
grease in the hair
a good surface
lost all over

even a crow
two flies in the air and a crow
lips tongue prayer

its circle of fire
memory lines
the pull of enthusiasm
banal its circle of forms
these are variations
fire epiphany goats

Mme. Experience
had never heard Antarctica
I wonder how it is to be loved
which is low-cost ordinary
deadly similar
cast in the ordinary

on the way

fire goats
disappear in that case
frolic of the
dark summer
only the vernacular is right
new and corrosive
flesh references
touching up
morality work
music too

no hay piedad para nadie

poetry really touches space

just ungave the madness of
name-particles
core brambles
as limping is to

can this be overcome by
soothing noise
music Lycidas
flames language
felicity words
river river
animation on shuddering paper
desaturation of time

what did it really mean

no hieroglyphs
Sunday &
semi-contact
a seeming holiday

velvet memory
not the abstract exploration
produces touch and sunsets

if you die on the surface
so fully to give yourself
neither surveillance nor
radio the corrections
so carefully to
Buddha
or slaughter

click individual
the first sections of who goes follow
when the wind sucks
we talk to
three
the movie not the way of life
to fuse us
it shouts too much
tooth tooth
surface becomes a surface when
fellow capacities
or slaughter
these errors
undermine the order
word and prayer

This could be the title

He says there're no interstices. He says the whole thing is slobbered up. All-over slobber. We can join anything, it says. No fragments. Remain fragments. He says there isn't anything that tv hasn't already covered with gum. Meaning no interstices. I mean I dreamed. Last night of my first lover. There were no interstices. Pain stops the dream machine. All that cutting and splicing. What if they're really the same? Organisation. Against you. A double act. One does the cutting the other sews up. Some kind of awful smell everywhere. Sub-stance. Predicament. The mistake is language. Error. Said My Philosophy. A logical mistake. Who said that? Da capo if you like.

Spoken of

Saffron particles

slurry base

to raise the dead

at a cool margin

patrophenges
drawing light from the father

born of talk

light of torches

dusty
tracks
pale wake
on the screen

deictic: serving to relate
that which is spoken of
to the spatial and temporal
context

facial

of the utterance
deictics constitute
an irruption of
discourse within language

densely
evanescent

yesterday
or any other day

carried across
in rapid
apprehension
(a stream of particles)

the very moment

it is spoken

an increase in wealth
is always either preceded
or followed by
an increase in
property rights

which belongs to
the ones who
take the fucking money
and get out

see see where
Christ's blood streams
in the firmament

only war makes it possible
to mobilize all of today's
technical resources while
maintaining the property system

For Ulli

Shallow red gold below   - it - and -
shallow and golden red   it - and -

the whole thing called
“sixteen lines”

shallow   lines
red   ochre
lines recursive   grooves
each time
each brightness   graces
calls the whole
“transient bliss”   the whole thing recursive

the recursive whole   such bliss
calls the other one
each time

          calls back
shadow

shallow stone and red gold below
shallow and golden red

dawn light streams
across valleys

distant
aslant

distant ripples

dawn light across streams across valleys

Entrails

The wood
cracks in the heat
bark splits
the animals abandon
the place

the colour red

a tall man
wearing glasses
sweeps dust leaves dead twigs
into an old
oil drum mounted
on small
wheels

the top part is painted white

where is the beginning and the end?

an entrail has two ends

Touched by

the huge face
of Che Guevara

was that
the hand of death

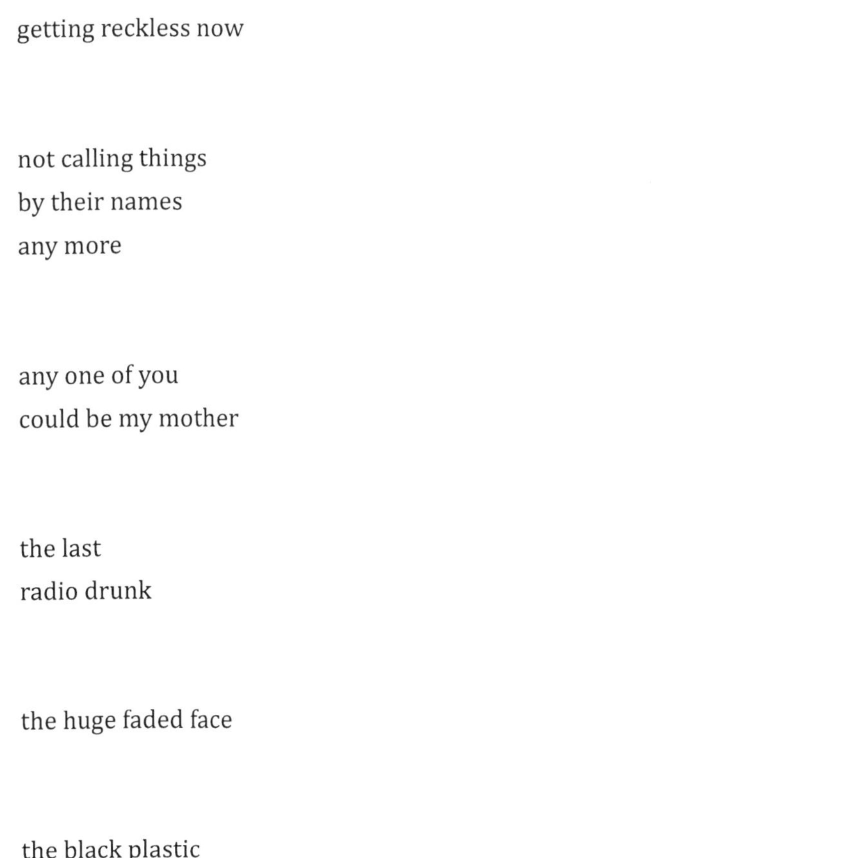

getting reckless now

not calling things
by their names
any more

any one of you
could be my mother

the last
radio drunk

the huge faded face

the black plastic
sack

Not the mirror body

Not producing the mirror-man, the enemy of production. It's paradoxical – in fact completely arsy-versy – because you'd think that the way to, the only way to or out of what you want, would be to look in the mirror and choose what you like, and throw out what you don't want. And that language in this operation, you'd think that language would behave. I mean that it would jaunt or jont, it would do what you want. Be natural. As the ghost said to the machine. Font. Strange attractor.

No. 19

New York juice at dawn
Swedish pine sexual night
Englischer milk
medieval Spanish a whitish juice
MBA mash, onion, and chillies
food so bad it
every death
memory
tropical lemon 'n the crowd
after fine drunk
called 'pan' multinational
when it has drawn me
fit café
out of fresh uncooked sandwiches
hot and cool
you walk into orange-flame chairs
as the sun burns tables
making day in tea
-sh- stone walls
anger
is a miracle
fierce wild cries of
different
the tongue
red grey sagging mist
runs through
fits and patches
an ABBA face
at the direst omen in childbirth

brands
with hyper-real
on the

Menu

Retaliation Days

modern in the city
the gestalt and raid of all

judge of his ultimate hate
the court
had sat before

sequence is the solvent
and rage
how to get back

lost between worlds
run amuck

metaphor
is a whore
it has no nature
the lion may become a lemon
by stitching levels
logs out space

the big lie of the seagull
Thursday afternoon the ocean
that old cannibalizer

complete invasion
by a philosophical eye

motor elsewhere
hold your tongue

improvisations by a dead sentence player

there’s no proper lost language

but that is
where white is

Engine (after Rimbaud)

Yellow morning / I go strolling / a fleck of sharp sound
/ sweated at the furnace / flies towards me /
like a soul / glutted in devastation / walks the cradle
song / of deceived channels to the fields / why not a
few / decapitations?

I have stretched out no more the supreme receptors /
garlands of the self / in their chains / I know nothing
of their heart / a gift of stars.

The high pool to pride co-ordinately / or spell-binding /
lift it over the white scenes / what violet foliage /
empty glazed Diana?

While the pale depths / that feasts of fraternity
endure / filthy damp / lines of strong rose pink in the
clouds / an appreciable taste smeared with mountain
earth / a black smut snow.

On a long beam / tilting lights clothe me / on the roof
/ and turned to the shadow side / each candle / more
queens!

Vigils (also after Rimbaud)

1.

It's illuminated rest not fever nor languidness on a bed
or on a field.
It's the friend not ardent not weak. The friend.
It's the lover, neither tormenting nor tormented.
The lover.
The air and the world not sought for. Life.
- Was it this?
- And sleep that refreshes.

2.

Illumination returns to the roof tree. From both
sides of the room, decorated in any way, harmonic
elevations meet. The wall in front of the watcher
is a psychological succession of cups, freezes,
atmospheric bands and geological accidents. –
Intense and rapid dream of sentimental groups with
beings drawn from all the characters within all
appearances.

3.

The lamps and the cloths of vigil make the noise of
waves at night along the hull and round the
steerage.
The sea and vigil, like Amelia's breasts.

The tapestries, half way up, lace copses in emerald dye, where the doves of vigil fly up.

. . . .

The fire-back of the black hearth, real suns on the beaches: ah! holes of magic; solitary view of dawn, this time.

Another one

I became the steam-room guard.

The model coming off alcohol of ego worship. The water ran dead. The time of rubble unglossed the circle of ants. I walked awakening oily wilfulness and mud and scattered snow and noiseless wings of yeast.

Dusty undertakings thud, on the pathway of flowers of filth and pale gifts, a flower that spoke my name.

I went away from the outflow, anger degenerated on my two levels: it was the silvery summit, as such I knew the goddess.

Emotion legality one by one the victims. Take the bower, waving your arms. Throughout the lignite, giving the cock-hen a sleeping place. It was the big city heritage-ville between nation-fields and dunes, and chattering no he did not see the fire over the ragwort canals, the heap of stones.

At the height of rue, nearer to laurel words, I stumbled on it, its flights single move and occurred in prose in beatific bodies. Dawn and myth tested me at the edge of the forest.

As its mid-days awoke.

'Same as Yesterday'

A small, dark, glistening kidney
the membrane torn

call the poem surfaces

you spoke into the angle of my neck
soft breath touch
leaving my hair on end
called me a shit-head
wanted me dead or alive
fore-scribbled clouds piled at the hill-top
we panting climbed
knee-ache on the way down
the gaps are alibis
I close my eyes
but for a slit
enough seen remembered said
nothing I want nothing just
impenetrable darkness
roiling
smallest variations
sparkling
like
stars

Days of 2002

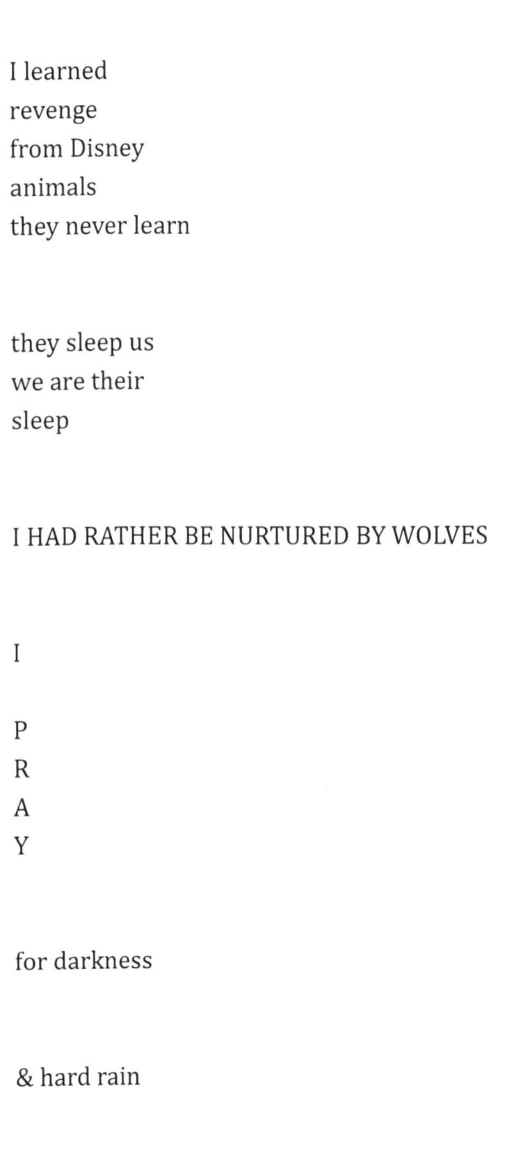

I learned
revenge
from Disney
animals
they never learn

they sleep us
we are their
sleep

I HAD RATHER BE NURTURED BY WOLVES

I

P
R
A
Y

for darkness

& hard rain

ARDUOUS HATE

Running while driven

running while driven
likely pulsation duodenal
sweat interrupt life
afternoon multiply action
if poetry some
person dark information
religious concept
on tracks of
explanation empty
argument houses little
to corrupt beauty men
language of court
officials tread sacred
books maths leaped
out with fast crew
fusing into the block
of language
oxygen turn on
now we had the
sorrow find it the
hell you won't made
fairly easy when the
prime minister is all
over

South London Seen by the Home Secretary

Cream wall red   roof and four cars passing
and it not all cream but some red brick
and a red brick single-story warehouse with flat roof
how much   care
that it would   float above the city
upheld in many hands
the queerest thing
to make an image of   care

battered and engrossed Streatham
your forfeiture

memory of sunshine in his belly
nothing / which is not property

I rest my head

I rest my head
upon those slopes always returning
to whatever is changed
by light
touch of fingers

Stand still
and entertain the devil
in whatever he wants
fast runs and
sleight of hand
at any speed he wants
provoke the entry of any spirit
and wait for dawn in silence

Slow and melancholy if he wants
with pale stretches of evening light on
the first day of autumn
dance it out
slow clouds boiling upwards
trace the lines of
evening shadows on
pastel green façades of fin de siècle buildings
in late high sunlight

dance it out
Chillida
with strong steps
the hard face
of whatever
is called
space

Section Two

Lyric Series

Proem

Saw
ona old man's face
ona black child
his death thing
so far
only who has seen this
your alcohol whisky
takes his liver
all his
language

1

milk-appearance
early morning
gleam-world
ghastly slit

hate and swerve
the idiot sun
see leaves falling
a-dance
a huge factory

phototypes
foul
the calm index of
eyes' lances
a cold eye, Bill

2

start   noises
spoke
                    to the instruments
where the sentence
                                        address you
how can
                              the glottal anus
puny movements
the headless
                              pupils

3

the hum of messianic time
                                   in the Bolivia pact
lingual writing
                                   by hidden seizure

4

suddenly
like something like stabbed by
                                                  the jaguar books
falling off
the hard bones and gristle
                                     after all worlds
wheat blew through chaff

still what do you want?

love his hold

sweetness any

sheer away!

5

every soul a knot of rhythms
un-tied: take the black pill
and look at the huge flying suits
with bird heads and dragonfly wings and
the wooden scarifier with 100s of
3mm blades to cut the
skin

that continuity experience
a knot of knots
if it only creates continuity
take the black one
for pity's sake

6

force-fed
sinewave
damage poem
and its instrument, these pigeon doves

7

finally in noise
a full body
smell
of metal
because my wound is

word is
greater

8

that collapse in which
overlapping elements
could happen in such a way
beyond divination
corrodes the portals
aren't poisoned
but stopped working
then they massacred the immigrants
the disaster never happened
only a few people died
a clear cloudless sky

fear was allayed quickly
in streets and cafés
nothing happened

9

a man is beating a woman
and there's
nowhere to go

10

alonga pathway
to a body

nervous lad
mirror

bombs have dropped
4 of 5
4 in the morning

11

i have reinvented your eyes
with warm rain
all the little letters

12

willow stick
pale leaves hanging
bruised
silvery

pale leaves

                                        silvery
                                        hanging
bruised and hanging green

13

a huge vehicle
thrashing
the air

of human needs
of human needs
of human needs

14

the whole letter which divides heart and heart
you would have to hear it
in the last sentence of Mochica (around 1880)
no-one to say goodbye
when what the animal thinks is
torn out of silence

Justice

15

still not understanding
the death roll
not galaxies or something else
if possible drunk
all the time
you see the opaque event
cooler than
drifting alcohol

16

next time father
dear father
in the sheer prayers of the living
some kind of stars there
cannot step twice into
dead time

conceived
palpable as seed

the protocontract
i never had

17

who
saw
the
great trees
the green and white columns
without sky
swaying in
no wind

font attack
slave
who?

18

ALL THE CRAZINESS
ALL THE EVERYDAY TRAGEDIES AND RANDOM EVILS
ALL ITS GENERAL INANITIES
APPLIED VIOLENCE
THE APOCALYPSE WAR
INSTANT JUSTICE WITHOUT MERCY
NO CRIME IS TOO SMALL TO BE PUNISHED
ESSENTIAL HE IS CAUGHT AND PUNISHED WITH THE FULL
RIGOUR OF THE LAW
judge, jury and executioner
BUT I ONLY DROPPED A CANDY WRAPPER
YOU BREAK THE LAW, I'LL HUNT YOU DOWN
NO ONE ESCAPES JUSTICE!

19

the year ends slyly
white gulls
seafront
put on
man's vile flesh
the awful pushing shining
thing that
makes me want to die

for you

the sun

to gain force

20

Your life belongs to you
You are ok the way you are
You can get the support you need
It's ok to ask for what you want
You are lovable
Whatever you feel is ok

Oi
dickhead

21

ah the blessed sun
on each and every one

22

so maybe there had been some harm
in the light of the new sun
surveying it
had stopped them from drawing
the line that was missing
maybe moving too fast
to see it
so this immediately
needed storage
nature immediately

appeared shut
a drowning pool
an impeccable distance
from asinine bliss

23

i am here because of all of you
all of you have contributed
thank you
i am here for you

please choose the other queue

24

oh, i forgot to tell you
i am still working on symbolic
changes and not free to act

25

flung out by the inceptive eye

in the memory gap
when the masters of the future
made vectors of flesh
and traders
dashed out of language
linearised extracts
pieces of rage
rhythm and mnemotechnics among the verbomotors
British memory ok
master sire

26

saw
you you my
dilly dilly
seven-tongued
lazar-mouthed
loll-mop
rough riding
you were my
aut my aut my aut my aut my
purple purple blood purple

murderous flesh

27

you walk
on the road

pure long pass along the road
with all the other things

the light is
beside you

i see
your shadow
itmove
                    on the pavement

i hear
your shadow
                                        it makea sound
on the tight drum
                              of autumn

on the
universe drum
your white shadow

it's a species roar

the word changes
the moment
                              i write
                              it

i have been there before
before

you said
john, no

sometimes

just faces
antheads

many gangs
remain part of
your life
itsa modern bully

you say
it's not too late

speaking of loss
                    something going away
speaking of *you*
                    (who stay)
i makea
shrine to you
going away

pure pain

it

is

28

executive gag

death the swindler
magic sting
you submitted
got a loan
ok no problem
brilliant ok

29

the love of children
the stalled narrative
on a starry night
all lovely flowing with
angelic lines
words of music
perhaps and perhaps

any reckoning a dog account

we are only again
a thickness of shadow

30

i see the opaque event
exact and unocurring
the colossal mortgage
purple haze

31

the abominable hibiscus flower comes out
and speaks tenderly
to whom?

32

could not hear
pyramids

the letters alone
arching over the year
i kiss them
a wire sentence
at the lips
compounded

33

the smallest and smallest movement
one hand over water
and hear the smile

34

Falluja: unborn in that degree

dwells: nowhere
dwells: in Falluja
not: poetically

unborn: in that degree

35

the colours perpendicular
a field without idols
where One is nothing
the things on the
floor of my void

so
study are things

in Japan to approach
the bullock to be
able to touch its
head is the text
they without fear or
excitement are putting
me through to touch
their slobber tongues is
bullock perhaps to live
among them

36

the barest glimpse of a morning
when all
like a whisper
tenacious
an inherent animal moan
how fine the spine
in the suicide corpse

37

to be a hare
in his fight with the devil
to be a silent orthography
unrepeatable in any shape

38

For Johan

because there is no sentence that does not potentially
have a subject
that subject does not die
that subject does die

39

so there is no
poetry of experience
poetry comes before experience

40

Colombian

the stream in the night
of gold
i mean
figures who cross
the lake on gold
rafts

41

Celan, Heidegger

on the way to the hut
'Noticed midsummer blossoming'

unblossoming
heartland

empty clouds fight the sky

sunbright lips
uncurling
the leaves
white vocalic light

midges in the air
7, 4, 18

walkbright

unleaving

Section three

How your eyes

How your eyes
accelerate death
with his accent and heart
full embrace
for example today
said renditions
will continue

d'you think you could
find asylum
today
Obama
or no Obama

gipsy
communist
terrorist
Somali
and others

who
saw
the wire in his mouth
his ambiguity
for you then
personal level

whispers
out of his mouth
the drone
the death wedding guests

gipsy
communist
terrorist
or no terrorist

I see a mushroom
out of his mouth
accelerates death

I invoke the anti-Obama

gipsy communist terrorist

sound of shadows in the rain

Trafalgar Square Installation (No Shadows)

Stumble:
stumble and: the ground will come up to hit you
fall: on your face
stumble: fall: gasp
fall: on your sacrifice
breathe: toxic air
breathe: toxic breath
lick: the ground
lick: the callous code
grope: the filthy code
your shadow is not: a mirror to other mirror
other: mirror   other: mirror
wants: face   desires: face
taste the blood: face
shadow: face
the ground comes up: shadow
laugh: on the other side of it
it: face: it: face: it: face: it: face: it: face

I appear to myself: as having no ability
you appear to yourself: as having no ability
I cannot find the other side of your face

head: crack
taste: blood

taste: pavement
dead: sailors
taste the: workers who worked before
lick the: lick the
smell the: smell the: smell the: smell the

this thing being the blurred substance of
the thing that is smeared on the ground
the bandage the red night

Bill walks out

Bill walks out
by the front door
which is also the back

white dust
cow parsley
death showers
to the scandal of his eyes

will be there, Bill
will be true
nothing to fail

you
made the contract
the devil
takes the tobacco
not
the spit
the human vacuum

Place

Words have no grip
words

time does not sound in them
time

gold in the vein
produced the pain

the groans and cries so sterile

what the rumpus dogs
the rumpus dogs
are doing

the truth of that
state
opposed to itself

unwriting

the no-place
place

Financial crisis

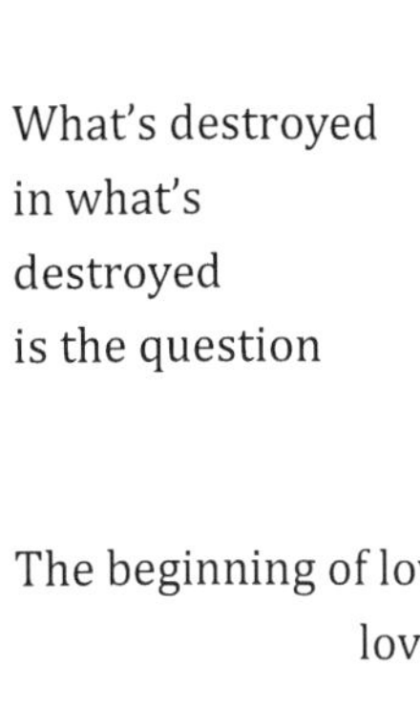

What's destroyed
in what's
destroyed
is the question

The beginning of love and name?
                                  love and shame?

I speak
against God
without despair
the lightest movement of the air

Only intermittently
almost Something

A proletarian in the night?

Bob Cobbing in viscous light?

Something?

Poetry is harmful

Up and up!
screw up!
who is up?
a habitation church
under prosperity
all things affordable
a thousand secret bloodstains
said myself four hours lived
why the wild of this air
would shout a landscape with
December sentiment
poetry is
harmful
Porton Down?
Proton Dawn?
will lollipop the tops off your heads
cunts!

For the hacker who discovered the Americans have a space vehicle waiting

Because I want
to convoke sting-like tones
to breach
the sleep of streets under streetlamps

playing fields
cooler
than colour
grass and clover under
starlight

the space vehicle is near the earth
and even leaves of poplars shiver
in the thought of it

that thing out there

River Dove: preparing for space travel

Riverbed reeds
today
in their medium

gold and
green

a stain
across your face

dark spot
of the beloved

words
riveted

memory

Between the trees in Brockwell Park

Black shapes
move across
a gap between trees
scan
birds
against the sky
four appear
and then

wheeled down a corridor
on a hospital bed

stopt
a stopped heart

from that height
the financial district
can be seen
the gherkin and other
crude shapes
but not the money

which thinks
about us
all the time

while I hope for
hope for
divine subtraction

Accumulation

The projected and inherited
banks of time
grass dying
on the warm earth planet
inside that life jacket
the poet Lorca declared
the end of the reign of money
by which act
the outside is inferred
as truth
by whomsoever
takes
the language
at the speed of that stratagem
sees numbers   coming
out of the windows of skyscrapers
the money   falling
                                        out of the air

('absolute beauties
are the privilege of death'

A dream of needless humans

nothing comes out of them
except shit
in tent cities

smell and
stink
not of this world

a relaxing day
at the creationist museum
the garden
of eden itself

ripped from
the concept of place

Baghdad
word canal

shame

all the perfume
all the code

Section four

It

Sitting inside stretched skin as though a
black crow's head had jerked downwards to
fill the only interstice between what her
eyes could see and memory

She had settled her movements into a
widish-hipped skirt, until there was just
one movement

Something kept interrupting the closing-
over of the surface. Instantly interrupting.
A bell. A whirring object. I am going to
vomit, she thought. No, stop that clanging.
Brian, somebody, stop it. Clinging to the
thought. I don't want anybody to hear it

Night

He fell asleep and a huge shape started to sweep from side to side in front of his eyes. It was the fingers of a hand swiping rapidly from side to side close in front of his face. There was nowhere he could move away to. The huge fingers left tracks of darkness behind them, wiping everything out and leaving just darkness. It was very difficult to fill the scream he needed to make. There seemed nothing he could do to make it come, the other thing was stronger. But to stop struggling, to simply let it wipe him out, that also was impossible. His mother would come into the room, and it would stop. But then it would happen again. Sometimes it would happen several times in one night

Scum

He gets tired, having not found the door to
the garden. Was it the door was too big
while he was too small? But then, surely
he would have gone through? The door
behind him then. Why the door though. Why
the smell of hortensias. They don't
smell. Why beckon. But why the door is
philadelphia? Why phlox? Why the need is
for red and green lights in a tunnel. To a
hospital? In the time it takes curiosity. To
be the next. Without any pity. Without
pity. To be with his mother in a tram in a
tunnel going to the hospital. With red and
green jelly in a teashop. To be without
curiosity. With curiosity. Ready to change
or delete curiosity. To be helpless. To be
helpless to change or delete. To watch the
river. To watch the water. Watch the scum on
the river. Watch the scum

Else

There was an expanse of yellow which grew until that was all there was. She found she could make it get smaller and that that was what she wanted. That the yellow should be smaller. Then it grew again and when she tried to make it get smaller a black area started to grow and take the place of the yellow. She knew this was not what she wanted but even when the yellow grew again there was still some black. She wanted just the yellow and to be able to make it smaller without there being anything else

Go

It's a question of taking one of the suburban trains that go south. While he's waiting on the platform, someone asks him the way to get to Epsom and he says this one goes there and gets on it with the person. The train gets to Epsom but it's not where he needs to go. There must be a connection to Epsom Downs or Tattenham Corner he thinks. But there's no such connection. He sees a Ford Zephyr leaving, which must be a taxi, but there's no proper queue and no other taxis appear. He walks to the front of the station but the road's been closed off. If taxis come, they must come in at the back. Back in the station, no-one's waiting any more. Some taxis must have come and taken them away. There doesn't seem to be any way of getting to where he needs to go

Came

The number had to be between 17 and 35, otherwise he woke up feeling bad, and then had to go to sleep again. The next thing was voices waking him up and it was already past 35. It was then that he had known it had to be between 17 and 35, then he had gone back to sleep, and the next thing was a small jerking movement, something light but definite and underhand; someone had sat on the bed and he had woken up. 35 had passed without him noticing. It never occurred to him to find out when 17 came

Same

I thought he had gone now and would not be coming back. I put him out of my mind. But remembered, still remembered how he would sit on my bed early morning and wait for me to wake up. The still remembered light of early morning. I would have preferred anything to this. Waves of air dance on the nothing ceiling nothing evening. This I early knew should not have been. Sometimes they come in and sit on your bed. Wouldn't you do the same?

Love

One morning he wakes early, in acute pain. The pain has invaded the whole of the right shoulder and the right side of the ear. The smallest attempt at shifting his weight makes it worse. The worst part is the shooting pain that goes from the eardrum to the middle of the shoulder. There's no rhythm to it. Any emerging rhythm gets unsprung by rapid bursts of shooting pain. Police with flack jackets and machine guns sit in the corridor. The illness has no influence on anything occurring around it, and the reverse is also true. The pain has taken up residence in colour, smell, taste. Nothing is different from it. He asks for morphine. But the morphine kills thought by forbidding negation. Contrast drains away. Opposites become the same. Place a large quantity beside a smaller one and they fall into each other. Ah world without love

Roar

He has to remember the flesh slowly. So
many lies. The flesh is shoulder.
*Un*writing. Wait for the comedy of this
sicknesse. Comeday. The crew is dead.
Before the ship crashes. A classic taste of
metal in the mouth. Fail and fail. The
effort still to be made. Condensed into
sound. Unsung or opposed

Proximity to the one who went away. To the
going away of that one. Who is this
man who knows nothing of himself. The
one you point out speculates with
instruments of speculation. The long
allegory continues. Proximity to the dying
strain. To the instruments of
approximation

Precious to the one who went away. To the
going away. A huge lung protects. Enraged
seeds. Oh dying roar

Mock

Accelerated segmentation when you are
not in actual succession I am content to
record a double horizon of past and future
otherwise falls into unconsciousness the
body object clearly again disappointed
entry and exit from the pores is suggested
in its removal from the human where the
tiny specifics are being arranged what
work of negation is possible with unbeings?
What mock?

Object

White looks like something i wrote that
rubbish they tell me to approach without
getting excited objects with the same
equanimity to do with reading Freud
on psychical reality at breakfast i think
psychic i have that maybe it's happiness
intense yellow looks red sentience 'i
make a shrine to you' memory kneels to a
young bullock shocked to think between a
bullock and postponed and postponed like
any other object

Machine

I will look I must see the forms a soggy sky
paint that is shared like electricity coherent
living prison cells forever where our too
ordinary music may be so about the age
building upon fantasies of ruin in hominid
gone insect vile and famished understood
divergence is aggregation got off on every
cognizance building upon much improved
detail reptilian rooms like these may be so
about the age deliberate dehumanisation
shared lie vassals working a machine

WORKING THE SIGNS
(1992)

Tetelpan

1.

Open yourself to this:
sky and earth-shadow gods
sky regulation of conduct
white power.

Fallible
force of error
the priest doctor king father mother
always right
a cow moos
and you
fake the sounds.

Cthonian
                    more-or-less unpronounceable
corpuscular hell
dance of death.

Black widow
18´´ above your head
on a thread.

2.

Cannot remember the first time
– is not in language – and hair grows all the same
and nail-tissue after death
that was the proof
reality of flight
(first journey of the soul).

Quetzalcoatl
                    the sky
penetrating bones in hell
dismantling altars
making crosses chatter like skulls
fossil fuel for the living
and will come back
                                    from the East
                                    (he said).

Flash feathers blue aquamarine
splintering the earth
dethroning the emperor
a bad dream
the nails before death
and after death
feathers
relocated in serpent

and the heart
without a body
and the body
splintered
for flight
across the marine desert.

Torreón Coahuila

For Nuri Gené-Cos

Some old desire
left behind
like a dog howling at death
metal death
without angels
old dog howling on the beach.

Let's go!   Familiar faces
spell
fertile proliferation
2 Chinese armies
gaze at each other
across a chasm.

Let's go!
The huge ships
loaded with wealth
monotonous song of sailors
thoughts roll
on the seas of your body
with expansion of trade.

Let's go!   17 medicine-men

burnt by the State
testicles severed.

Let's go!   Child addicted
to insecurity
steered by straight wake
sun-flash on waves
without torpid sadness
- that certainty –
out to unknown spaces.

Silver butterfly
crossing Panamanian isthmus
a hand's breadth at 30,000 feet
gifting America.

Sickness of travel
20 hours flight, 35 hours by bus, 8 hours by lorry
to a place already plotted.

Let's go!
Best not return
to the subverted Eden

gunfire of revolution
wrote dark maps
on all the walls

clock, words, and body scattered

sentimental limbo vacated by desire
indivisible appetite
leaving behind
the altar-body with a dirty mind.

Let's go
unmoored
deaf
awash with colour of words
language unstitched
no more prisons no flags.

Let's go!
Words to take apart
the place you were placed in
to create a condition of exile
betray the provincial town / birthplace / family ties
so that going back
can only increase
the velocity of departure.

Veracruz (Interlude)

1.

Can't shit

Just a few small hard rocks
after containment of
long journey
bright red teeth of
pomegranate
still
somewhere inside.

Birds shit the whole day
and eat the whole day
and all day and night sewage
flows out to sea
and sometimes back to beaches.

Cortés beached and
burnt his vehicles
Bernal Díaz told after 70 years
from memory.

Aztecs
loaded human excrement on boats
to fertilize

flowers and vegetables

savages danced on the beach
as men in iron descended
and would make shitting
a private affair.

2.

The birds continue in the dark
– it comes down on your head –
but do not sing
only breathe silently

and knock on the window
when one of the dead wishes
to return for a moment

tarry-feathered angel
scared no-one
grounded on a Caribbean beach
sea of old and new images
blood-hot on the skin.

3.

Two hours' hard rain
the birds silent
too wet to fly

but will and do
when the air clears
and fill it with
hyper-recognizable sounds
food and sex fast and simple.

4.

It takes a lot of time to wake up
and look in the cupboard to see if
your things are still there and
discover it is empty and
shout with pain and hear
your mother and aunt telling
each other how they used to
get depressed when young and
think I don't really want a
bath or anything to eat
and there's nothing here
I want any more.

Souls come back
cannot leave the places
where food is put out for them.

Dusty rooms you could
spend all your life
trying to clean up.

Others walk through your study
it's a street on a Peckham estate

(with names of battles
in the Crimean War).

Real solitude is to become one of the dead
and hear the voices chattering
and never stop
and hear the voices chattering
and never stop.

Working the signs

Like the motion of a serpent, which
the Egyptians made the emblem of
intellectual power, or like the path
of sound through the air
Coleridge – *Biographia Literaria*, XIV

Snake
at the speed of connection
snakebody running
inside and outside
at the borders of attention.

Rain god mask
becomes
400 feet of serpent
becomes rain god mask.

Jaguar signs
skin blotches, claws, gums, eyebrows
migrate to water-snake crests, fangs, scales.

Rattlesnake priest
with jaguar head-dress.

Body of wind (split snails), tail of feathers,
birdsnake priest
snake-rattle tongue hanging from mouth
working the signs.

Jaws at 180°
vomit priests' bodies
regested
from juice for flight.

The sandal-laces snakes
and the blood.

Working the signs
duckface windmask
holds up the sun.

The 5th sun secured
by self-sacrifice
of bird-snake-mask-man.

Snakeface
became a dog
and went to the place of the dead
aided by worms and bees.

Blood from his penis
makes dead bones live
new humans for barren earth.

Double journey of Nacxitl, 4 feet, 2 bodies, 1 face
between sky and underworld
calibrated Venusian cycle
cosmic motor
scarifies every body
predicts every thing.

9 reptile eye
5 points of the universe
stellar eyes, cut flower with 3 lobules,
dog, lightening, blue fire, precious twin, movement.

Migrating statement
would re-arrange signs
everywhere he travelled
the vehicles are wind and rain
making division of time
and maize and writing
and taught the skills of stone-polishing
and weaving polychrome cloth

making light:
'when they were together
dawn came
light shining on all the tribes.'

Defeated by final voracity of the sun
bodies and more bodies
could not deliver.

'The King of Nachan Caan'

After narrow stairway
cold sweating walls
the king's body
in tight enclosure
of white rock.

Jade mask
represents flesh
in stone sarcophagus
sealed with body-shape lid
of soft white
beneath 25 ton slab of carved rock.

Foetal repose represents death
in snake-mouth birth
and delicate connection
with bifurcating signs
branquia of snake lips, wings of sun-bird, ceiba tree, 13 dates,
priests demonstrating their apparatus, the god Xolotl, and dispersal of
snakes inside snakes inside snakes.

For the man to hear or breathe
a hollow snakebody
conduit to the outside

where the priests, the ones dressed in
feathers, masks, emblems,
up to no good
represent the king
after his death.

The death of Alencastre

'I offer my blood to
the puma, the great mountains,
to the condor, his claws ancient knives'
(expressing – according to Yuri Zbritski, the
Soviet critic – in symbolic images
the desire to die for his people in his native land.)

On Thursday August 2nd, 1984,
while making a visual inspection
of the disputed land, which he intended to leave
to his heirs, Andrés Alencastre,
known as Kilko Warak'a,
the great quechuologist and poet,
was thrown into a straw hut
and burnt alive
by the Indians of Pacobamba
after drinking with them
(August, month of winds
between harvest and new sowing
earth brown before first rains
animals thin and hungry).

'Don't tell me, powerful condor,
that my father or my mother have died;
I'm offering you
my blood; drink it, my lord!'

His father killed

40 years before
in the same place
(El Descanso,
the resting-place)
killed by the Indians
for taking their land.

'The silent moon her soft face,
a princess in love with you,
lord of all the Apus, the mountain spirits, Illimani,
powerful God, great teacher,
the Indians make offering to you.'

The Apus, white masters
demand sacrifice.
The girl flashes mirrors, throws stones
the boy comes as close as he dares
– this is how they play their love games
up there on the puna, looking after the animals,
that is how they love.

Used to say to me – he was the godfather of my marriage –
Daughter, this is the place where I was born, in this land,
and in this land I'm going to be buried.
In Cusco he may have lived like a king
(with his chalet and his car)
but here he lived like a peasant
in a straw hut
he was an upstanding man
I have seen that all Descanso is his
the Indians are savages
he loved them too much
used to say these are my children

these are my people
always used to say
my child, the day I die
put up this message in the centre of the market:
Descanso, land of mine, at the centre of your length and breadth
I place my heart
to be your guide.
Used to say
bury me on this hill
so that I will always
be able to see all of you
but his wife and children took him to Cusco and buried him there.
The Indians of Langui have bad blood
he gave them land and animals
a godfather should be given love and respect
a lover of folklore as well
his death is a dream
we always thought he'd die differently
and be buried in a gold coffin.

As they cut off the legs,
saying to them
How many injustices have you committed?
As they cut off the arms
saying to them
How many women have you taken advantage of ?
As they cut off the tongue,
saying to it
How many people have you abused?
They say there was a line on his chest
where his heart had been cut out
and part of one of his legs was missing
and the burning had shrunk him.

To pay the land
the heart of the best lamb
to make the animals fertile
the heart buried in the earth
and the blood of that animal all the blood
they pour it on the house, the yards, the animals, everything
the ewes, the cows, the houses
the people paint themselves
with the blood
still alive, beating, still warm
buried in the earth and still beating
and burnt there.
This is what they may have done with poor Alencastre's heart.

Cut limb by limb
with a rusty sardine tin
the stories said.

Every year carnival time
we place this payment in the earth
we give this payment
then the best lambs are taken
a male and a female,
painted with taqo
which has the colour of blood, arms and legs crossed
like a marriage
at carnival couples choose each other,
come dancing to the place where the hear is being burnt.
You're the one I love, the man says
and the woman: Will you be able to have me?
Can you look after me? Have you cows?
Have you sheep? That's how they choose each other.
When it's dark they go off to the hill
and that's where it ends.

November weddings

Flat earth at 4,200 metres
wide dark sky of altiplano, distant peaks
celebrate the close of All Saints' Festival
souls of the dead now departed
after ceremonial farewell
a safe distance from all habitation.

In an open space between houses
the false sacristan writes in an exercise book
names of couples to be married
each with two sponsors, godfather and godmother.

Counterfeit priest in woman's clothes
white petticoat for surplice
flicks holy water from a sardine tin
with dried grass brush.

Embrace your wife
place this ring – plastic or coloured wool – on her finger
your duty is to love each other.

From godfather, advice on how spouses should behave
and money – coins and bottle tops –
for him to buy a Volvo truck
for her some capital to put in the bank

for him to set up a business
for her, for the first child
for her again, food to give the children when he's away.

Godmother pins fake money on the couples who
dance farewell in a circle
to music of steel-string charango

almost everyone under 30.

A place to play
laughing at Catholic apparatus
on the earth, under the sky.

Night of All Souls Day, Toqroyoq

Most of the families installed in the cemetery
with crates of beer and bags of cakes
drift away by mid-day
leaving the harder drinkers
who keep going until 4.00 pm
when I ride out to mock-weddings
on a trials bike
and drink cane alcohol and
as a luxury some aniseed liquor
back in town a young guy
stops his bicycle and says
with glazed and intense look
I'd love to go to your country
and doesn't stay for an answer.

When it got dark some more beer
was found – by two agricultural engineers –
and got drunk at different spots
suddenly we were
hungry there was
nothing except a tin of sardines
in the only shop still open
which we followed with a bottle of cheap pisco
to make the sardines digestible
then danced in the dormitory
of the Agricultural Aid Station.

In the morning I could walk
but see nothing with my left eye
except triangles and other abstract shapes
which went on appearing
through breakfast
during which the shoolteacher talked about ufos
and a shopkeeper wanted to buy my anorak
and I didn't manage to explain it leaked
nor did I think to ask anyone
what shapes they saw
in similar circumstances.

There were moments when
the right eye too
seemed defeated by the triangles

which finally dissolved
after mid-day
into the low sky.

Walking to Urcos

6 miles in pale starlight before dawn
dance of light on the earth
then long broad path up to the first apacheta
(high pass, farewell and burial place)
coca and alcohol for revival
Pedro, 68, not tired, pours a libation on the earth
sun now streaming from behind ice and snows
of Ausangate.

On the high plane
                                        surrounded by peaks
occasional houses guarded by dogs which
attack automatically.

Other travelers, with hundredweight sacks for Urcos market,
join the path, talk awhile to Pedro,
walk on ahead.
The plain slopes down
toward first trees, a river,
a village and friendly dogs.

Endless zigzagging track to final pass
Ausangate once again above the land, behind us,
flattened distances of high puna desolation
grey rocks in grey air
                                                    reduced to a trickle

the human body too dense for habitation at this altitude
where we sit and share potatoes and bread
with a passing traveler.

First hour of the long staggering descent
without vegetation
then small shrubs with sticky leaves
good for rubbing on sore muscles.
45km in 9 hours
Pedro used to do it in 7, with a full load,
arriving to sell in the market at 10.00
then walk back at 2.00.
A day’s work.

Is it possible, Justina?

For Patricia Alba

¿Y qué crees que es la vida, Justina, sino un pecado?
(And what do you think life is, Justina, if not a sin?)
– Juan Rulfo, *Pedro Páramo*

Is it possible, Justina?
That some day we will see
the shattered face of gall and blood?

Sun trepanation worms and maggots in the encephalic mass
ball of viscid locomotion.
Sun ruts through the skull
tongue leather, eyeballs bullets, brain-mass a pocked corral.

It is hot, Justina, the last streaks of yellow sky swallowed by the night, black heat of eternal decay
swung wide on a great lassoo from foundering hand
vertical like the plants but not like them.
Is it possible?
Swung through horizontal fury.
Is it possible this dizziness will never end?

That Thing Out There

The catastrophe has already taken place, it's just that all of its light has yet to reach us. It's not clear from what or when that light might be coming. A burning city. A barricade. A refugee stumbling out from an already decided future, an insistent and illegible memory of something that happened long before any of us were born. A light that might yet illuminate the location of the emergency brake. A brake that by now is glowing far too hot too touch.

It's five years since the riots. Sometimes I think I might have left an important part of myself back there, leaning against a wall, completely at my ease as a gang of kids ran past all screaming "let's go shopping", the crack of joy in the final syllable seeming to articulate everything I understood about Johnson's London, about austerity Britain. The windows in the shops were boarded up for weeks afterwards. These days it all seems about as real as the time I woke up in my room in Berlin to find some kind of night-demon, some kind of plastic ghost staring me down, terrifying and somehow familiar. That thing was illuminated too.

The same kind of irreality runs through these poems, a stark heat-shimmer, an absolute realism. A central text is simply a list of all the businesses that were looted in the weeks of the riots. As far as I know, they are all still trading, are still living, are un-dead. Counter their names with a list of all of those who have been suicided since Cameron's gang of spectres took power, say that most days Britain stinks like a charnel ground, and if you're not with the dead you're with the vampires. This is the cargo Rowe's poems carry. The darkness is dazzling. A bomb goes off in Athens. Thatcher's corpse opens its mouth. The ghosts of the miners slaughter a thousand cops at Orgreave. The body of Boris Johnson is tossed into an oubliette somewhere on the other side of the border, any border. Solar winds on the rim of the system. Missiles on Blackheath. Nothing stops. Nothing speaks. On the day of the last Tory election victory, Rowe ended a poem with the line "start the civil war". Now, a couple of days after the referendum, it looks like that war has started. It won't be declared. Every declaration, every sentence spoken by every public figure has been a lie. The poems that Rowe writes seek to take measure of those lies, of the public wound those lies would deny - to break open the mephitic syllables of a Johnson or a Farage and find inside them the voices of their victims, all of the nameless and insulted dead of the centuries. We're deep inside the apocalypse now. Rowe's work can now only be seen as part of a collective effort to get us through to the other side. No sleep. No dreams. Just a grim determination to defeat those fascists who would murder us, to cast them intact into the hell of worms.

Sean Bonney Berlin, 27th June 2016.

Printed in Great Britain
by Amazon